Fanny at Chez Panisse

Fanny at Chez Panisse

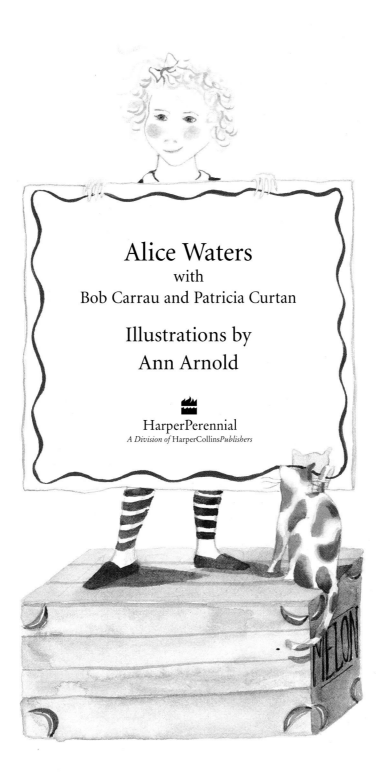

Alice Waters

with

Bob Carrau and Patricia Curtan

Illustrations by

Ann Arnold

HarperPerennial

A Division of HarperCollins*Publishers*

for Tom Guernsey

First HarperPerennial edition published 1997.

Designed by Patricia Curtan

The Library of Congress has catalogued the hardcover edition as follows:

Waters, Alice.
    Fanny at Chez Panisse / Alice Waters, with Bob Carrau and Patricia Curtan ; illustrations by Anne Arnold. — 1st ed.
        p. cm.
    Includes index.
    ISBN 0-06-016896-X
    Summary: Seven-year-old Fanny describes her adventures with food and cooking at her mother's restaurant in Berkeley, California. Includes forty-two recipes.
    1. Cookery—Juvenile literature. 2. Chez Panisse—Juvenile literature. [1. Cookery.
2. Chez Panisse. 3. Restaurants, lunch rooms, etc.] I. Carrau, Bob. II. Curtan, Patricia.
III. Arnold, Ann, ill. IV. Title.
TX652.5.W359 1992
647.95794'67—dc20   92-52586
                                                                       AC

ISBN 0-06-092868-9 (pbk.)

13 14 15 ❖ 10

Contents

Fanny's Restaurant Stories

Sometimes when my mom picks me up from school, I can tell right away we're not going home. "There's been a little emergency," she says. "We need to get a few things for tonight's dinner at the restaurant." My mom thinks everything's an emergency. If the tomatoes aren't ripe, that's an emergency. If the fish isn't fresh, that's an emergency. If the cooks aren't happy, that's an emergency. If there's not enough garlic, well, that's a real emergency. We drive all over Berkeley and make millions of stops. We go to the bakery and get bread. We go to the fish store and get whatever just came in. We go to the vegetable market, the butcher, the cheese store, the place that sells olive oil and spices, the vinegar maker, the fruit stand, the herb and salad garden . . . Like I said, lots of stops. We end up with so much stuff in our car that sometimes I feel like I'm in the middle of this driving stew. And then my mom sees some wild fennel or mustard growing in a vacant lot and we have to stop and pick some of that and get away before someone sees us. When we finally get to Chez Panisse, I'm always afraid we're going to open our car doors and everything is going to spill out all over Shattuck Avenue.

Oh, I almost forgot! My name is Fanny and Chez Panisse is a restaurant in Berkeley run by my mom and about a hundred of her friends. Chez Panisse means "Panisse's house" in French. Fanny just means Fanny. My mom got both our names from an old French movie about a girl named Fanny who marries a nice old man named Panisse. The movies always make my mom laugh and cry. I can make my mom laugh and cry, too, but it's not quite the same.

The restaurant really is in a house. There's a café upstairs and a restaurant downstairs. Each has its own kitchen with a brick oven, lots of counters, and a big stove where you can put twelve pots on at once. When I was really little, my mom used to stick me in the empty stock-pots sitting on the counter. They were just like little playpens for me. I used to stand up in them and watch everything that was going on in the kitchen. People would come by and give me treats. Mary Jo would give me strawberries. Peggy would pop me a little pea. Tom would come by and cackle and pinch my bottom (I didn't like that) and, sometimes, I'd even try and hide in the bottom of the pot so my mom couldn't find me or so I could jump up and surprise people when they walked by.

My mom and dad take me to eat in the café upstairs at least once or twice a week. Everyone is always real busy, but no one is too busy to say, "Hey, Fanny!" I start swimming in the smells that go right into my nose and shoot up into the part of my brain that likes tasty smells.

I usually see Fritz first. He's a maître d' and wears bow ties and knows lots of jokes. This is one of Fritz's jokes: "Did you hear about the restaurant on the moon? Great food. No atmosphere." Fritz's best joke is when he tells my mom he doesn't have a table for her.

I draw all over the paper tablecloth while my mom orders dinner. She always says something like, "I think we'll try the oysters on the half shell with mignonette sauce to start, the Hawaiian swordfish with bread crumbs, the garlic-roasted potatoes, and the pasta with wild mushrooms. Oh, and the garden salad, too, please." The inside of my mom's mouth knows how everything at Chez Panisse is supposed to taste. Usually, I just have pizza.

Michele, the pizza chef, is a friend of mine. He wears a white golf cap and is always glad to see me. I tell him, "I'm here to make pizza, Michele," and he gives me a piece of dough. I squish it out on the counter and flatten it out with all my fingers. It doesn't have to be perfectly round but it does have to be just right. Rolling out the dough is the hardest part. It takes lots of pressure and muscle. After Michele twirls the pizza in the air, we press it back down on the counter and add garlic, olive oil, tomatoes, mozzarella cheese, and whatever else is around that looks good. Then it goes in the oven to cook on the hot bricks. One time I made a pizza in the shape of an olive oil bottle and decorated it with olives.

My friend Maud and I tried to fool Michele once by telling him we were both Fanny. He said he could figure out who the real Fanny was because he knew exactly what she liked to eat. So, first he gave us both these salty, vinegary olives and we both ate those, no problem. Then he gave us a little bit of anchovy—that was harder because I know people don't usually like anchovies and I only like them on Caesar salad. But we still both ate them and Michele was still fooled.

Finally, he sliced a clove of raw garlic in half and gave us each a piece. I said, "It's no problem, Michele," because my mom always told me, "If you're sick you should always eat a whole clove of garlic and then you'll feel better." But when we popped those big raw pieces between our teeth, both our faces turned bright red, our eyes watered, and it felt like fire was in our mouths. We fell over like dead rats and then raced to the ice machine. Michele laughed, and Maud said, "From now on, you can be Fanny all by yourself!"

It's different downstairs at the restaurant. There's only one menu
to eat and no one has any choice. You have to eat all five courses. Sometimes people come and say, "I don't like peppers! I don't eat garlic! I
don't like fish like that!" It reminds me of me whenever my mom or dad
want me to try something new. I always put up a fight. Like one time,
my mom was trying to get me to eat halibut cooked in fig leaves and I
said, "What? Halibut cooked in fig leaves? Are you kidding? Yuck! I
don't want it! I don't want it! I don't want it!" And she said, "Just try
one bite! Just try one bite! Just try one bite!" And I said, "I don't want it!
I don't want it! I don't want it!"

And she said, "I'll bet you like it! I'll bet you like it! I'll bet you like it! It tastes sweet, just like a coconut." "I don't want it! I don't want it! I don't want it!" "Remember the time you said you didn't like ricotta cheese on your pasta, you only liked Parmesan?" "Yeah." "And then you tried just a little bit and ricotta became your favorite cheese?" "Okay, I'll try some. But just a little bit." So I put the fish in my mouth and guess what? It tasted way better than I thought it would and I ate it all up.

Everybody has something they like or don't like. I mean, I love plum ice cream but I hate fat on meat or capers on anything. I remember my mom's friend Marion used to bring her husband Robert to the restaurant and he didn't like to eat anything. He only came because Marion loved to eat there, and every time he came he would say, "Just give me steak and potatoes. Don't give me anything else." One night the cooks really fooled Robert. They were cooking these fried pigs' ears and they looked just like one of his favorite dishes—pounded steak that was breaded and fried. Bill took the plate out to him and nobody said anything. The cooks watched from the kitchen as Robert ate every bite. After he was done, they went over and asked him, "How did you like it?" Robert sat back in his chair and said, "That was the most delicious breaded steak I've ever had." Everyone started laughing and when they told him what he'd really just eaten Robert turned white and nearly fell over in his chair but then had to admit that he had liked it. I told him we'd change the names on the menu every time he came after that so he'd never know what he was eating. "You better not," Robert said.

I don't even know why they write menus ahead of time because they always end up changing everything at the last minute. Paul, the fish man, calls and says, "There's a storm out at sea and they couldn't fish for halibut but I've got some feisty live crabs." Or Ina calls from her farm and says, "We're picking beans today, can we send you some?" Or Jeff calls and says, "Sorry, I couldn't find any mushrooms today. They were there last week but since we haven't had any rain they all disappeared." So, right then and there, all the cooks—Paul, Jeff, Michael, Jerome, Alan, and Seen—change everything. They put the fresh crab in the pasta instead of the soup, and they put the beans in the soup instead of the salad, and they put cheese in the salad where the beans were supposed to be. It gets really crazy but I like it this way because every dinner turns out to be a surprise. Besides, I don't like wild mushrooms that much to begin with.

I like to be around on Wednesdays because that's the one day the vegetables come in from the Chinos' farm way down in Rancho Santa Fe. The Chino family has the most beautiful farm in the world. There are just rows and rows of every sort of vegetable and they all look like

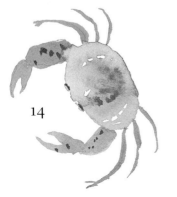

jewels. You never know exactly what the Chinos are going to send so opening the boxes is like opening a big surprise treasure chest. Sometimes there are striped tomatoes or yellow ones with orange veins or little tiny mini-red tomatoes that are littler than peas. Sometimes there are all these different color peppers that are every color of the rainbow. Sometimes there are even brown ones. In the summer there's big and little corn and all different color basils or beets or whatever else the Chinos have been growing. The cooks always stop whatever they're doing when the Chino boxes arrive and dive into them, smelling and sniffing and saying, "Taste these peas! They're so sweet!" Or, "What is this, a turnip?" Or, "Look! These carrots are white! I've never seen a white carrot before! Have you?!" Or, "Smell these basils! This one smells like lemon! This one smells like cinnamon! This one smells like lime!" Or, "Look at these white eggplants! They look just like eggs!"

P.S. Do you think that's where eggplant got its name? From the Chinos' small white eggplants?

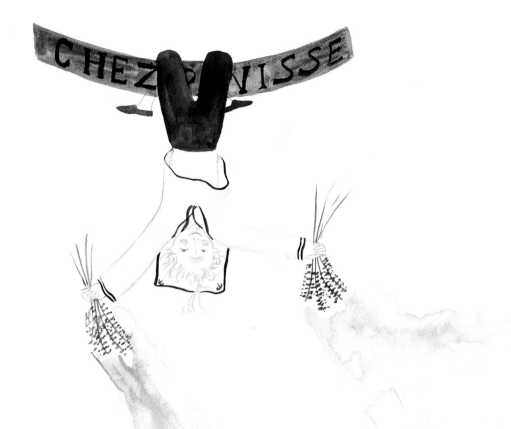

There are always fires going in the kitchens of the restaurant.
Sometimes, so much smoke from the fires goes out the chimneys that
my mom worries the fire department might come. But if they did, they
wouldn't find a fire. Nope, they would find lobsters grilling on seaweed
or maybe rows of chickens turning on a spit in front of the flames or
maybe just some almonds roasting in a pan. Sometimes you can smell
what's cooking at the restaurant way down the block.

People all over the neighborhood smell the pizzas in the pizza oven
and say, "What is that? I'm hungry." Sometimes I think the smells of
bread and roasting meat pull people into the restaurant like little smoke
fingers and, when there's nothing cooking in the ovens, my mom and I
try to keep the smells going by lighting branches of rosemary and wav-
ing them around like incense in the garden out front. People passing by
on the sidewalk stop and sniff and think, "Hmmm . . . maybe we should
have lunch."

A very scary thing happened after they put the new grill in downstairs. Someone was pouring the charcoal into the fire and a little spark got into the bag of mesquite charcoal and nobody saw it. In the middle of the night, when the restaurant was closed and no one was there, the spark caught all the other charcoal on fire and the restaurant started to burn. My mom got a phone call and rushed over and saw flames coming out of the windows and firemen running everywhere trying to put the huge fire out. No one got hurt, but after it was over everything was burned and black.

People were very upset after the fire. Everyone was afraid the restaurant might never open again. Hundreds of customers wrote letters that said things like, "You can't close Chez Panisse, we had our wedding dinner there." Or, "When I lived in Berkeley I had lunch in your café every Thursday," Or, "We celebrated our children's graduations at your place!" And so many people helped that the restaurant got rebuilt even better than it was. I'm glad it did, too, because now I have a place where I can invite all my friends up from school to have pizza parties or run up and down the stairs or play hide-and-seek in the front courtyard.

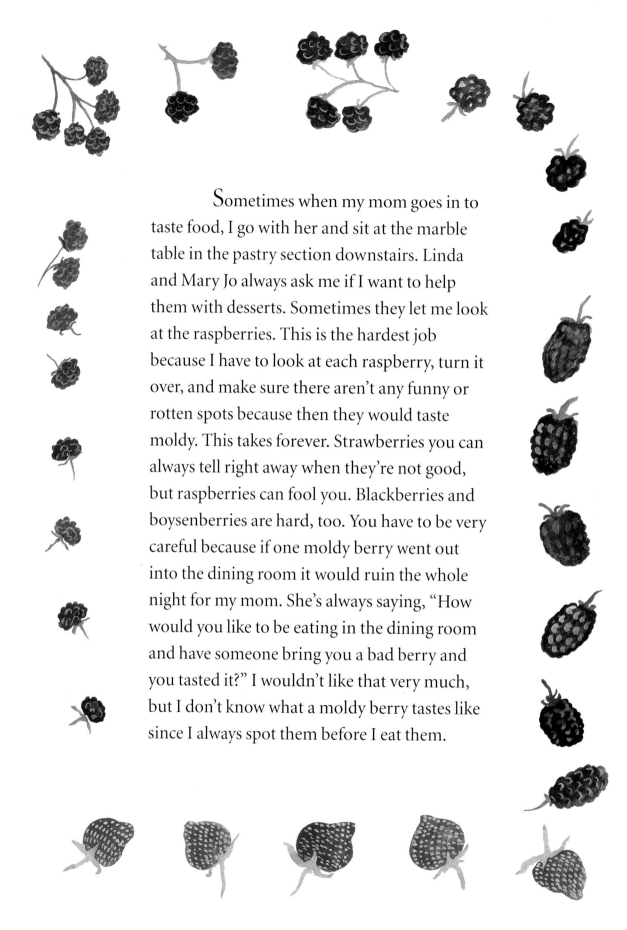

Sometimes when my mom goes in to taste food, I go with her and sit at the marble table in the pastry section downstairs. Linda and Mary Jo always ask me if I want to help them with desserts. Sometimes they let me look at the raspberries. This is the hardest job because I have to look at each raspberry, turn it over, and make sure there aren't any funny or rotten spots because then they would taste moldy. This takes forever. Strawberries you can always tell right away when they're not good, but raspberries can fool you. Blackberries and boysenberries are hard, too. You have to be very careful because if one moldy berry went out into the dining room it would ruin the whole night for my mom. She's always saying, "How would you like to be eating in the dining room and have someone bring you a bad berry and you tasted it?" I wouldn't like that very much, but I don't know what a moldy berry tastes like since I always spot them before I eat them.

You never have to worry about Mr. Hadsell's raspberries. Every year he says he's not going to grow them anymore because he's getting too old. But every summer his wife drives him to the restaurant from their house in Orinda with a box of them that he's grown in his backyard. Mr. Hadsell picks them all himself and carefully carries them into the restaurant, and every one is perfect. We never even have to look at them, and we never put them in the refrigerator. We just serve them quickly at lunchtime, and they're so sweet we never have to put sugar on them. Sometimes Mr. Hadsell stays for lunch but usually he doesn't. He once had some plums called Howard's Miracles that were so juicy I couldn't even chew them without the juice dripping all down my clothes. Wouldn't it be funny if Mr. Hadsell's first name was Howard?

Lindsey is the pastry chef and my mom's partner. She makes the best desserts in the whole world. She likes to make them one at a time like each one was the most special one or something. She actually knows how to make tarts and ice cream and candy from *real flowers*. Lindsey used to make cakes in a little cottage behind the restaurant before they made the kitchen bigger. She would bring them over right before they were supposed to be served. Sometimes, when it was raining, Lindsey would race over carrying a cake in one hand and an umbrella in another. Lindsey really needs my help when she makes violet ice cream. We have to pick hundreds of violets from her dad's garden. Then we have to separate the blossoms from the stems and the leaves. It takes forever! Once I even helped Lindsey pick wild plums at her mother's house for some wild plum ice cream sandwiches. It took us forever to squeeze the balls of ice cream between the gingersnaps, but boy did they taste good!

P.S. When Lindsey leaves notes for her cooks, she writes them on little pieces of paper using little handwriting that goes all over the page, up and down, front and back, on the sides, and upside-down. That's how I write letters to my friends—all over the place—so I can read everything Lindsey has to say.

There's an old yellow cat who lives on the back porch of Chez Panisse. We call her Mama Cat. Mama Cat must be extremely old because she's been there ever since before I was born. No one knows why she stays because it gets so crazy with busboys running up and down the back stairs and delivery men making deliveries and charcoal and wood being loaded into the kitchen and crates of fish and wine rolling by. But I know why she stays. Because everyone feeds her the most tastiest snacks all the time. At least twenty times a day someone comes by and says, "Hello, Mama Cat. Are you hungry? Do you want something to eat?" And Mama Cat always meows so they give her chopped-up fresh tuna or little pigeon livers or a little tidbit of crab cake—whatever they can find in a rush in the walk-in. But secretly, I think she's meowing for another reason. I think it's because she wants to be petted. So I always pet her and she likes that a lot.

A couple of weeks ago someone was eating in the dining room and their baby was screaming. My mom said, "Those people can't be enjoying their dinner. I'll go and see if I can help." So she went to their table and offered to hold their baby while they ate. The parents said, "Okay," and my mom took the baby into the kitchen but it was still crying and no one knew what to do. I remembered right away what my mom did with me when I was a little baby and I would cry at the restaurant. "Let's get the biggest bowl in the kitchen," I said. So Janet got the big salad bowl down from the shelf and we put the crying baby into it, blankets and all. We turned the bowl around and around under the lights and, sure enough, just like I used to, the baby liked the feeling and stopped crying. I thought it would be funny to put some salad in the bowl with the baby and so I got some little lettuces from Catherine and put them in the bowl with the baby. The baby liked this even more and looked really delicious with the lettuce leaves all around it. But, just then, the baby's mom and dad came in the kitchen and saw what we were doing. They told us, "Thanks a lot," but I'm still not sure if they liked having their baby look like a salad.

My mom's favorite thing is salad. She said if she had a kid who wouldn't eat salad she wouldn't know what to do. Luckily, she has me. I love salad. Especially red oak leaf and romaine and spinach. I eat my salad by picking each leaf up and wrapping it around a garlic crouton. It makes the salad like a sandwich. Then I rub my lettuce crouton in the bottom of the bowl to get as much oil and vinegar as I can on it. Then I pop it in my mouth! People see me eating my salad with my hands and say, "Why isn't she using her fork?" Sometimes you do have to use a spoon or fork, like when you're eating ice cream or mashed potatoes or cereal. But sometimes eating with your hands is the best way, like when you have a leg of chicken or a pizza or a big bowl of cherries. There are some things that are hard to make your mind up about like pasta or vegetables but I always say, "When in doubt, use your hands."

When I go to the restaurant really early in the morning, the first thing I see people doing is washing lettuce and making pasta. They do it every day. My mom says they're the most important jobs at Chez Panisse. She says, "If the salad and the pasta aren't right, then nothing's right." Mustafa lets me help him sometimes. My favorite part is putting the dough into the roller, because you put it through and through and through and it comes out in these long strips. I think the people who make the pasta and the salad always wish they were cooking at the stove but, to me, washing salad and making pasta is cooking because those are my favorite things to eat.

P.S. Whatever you do, don't stick your fingers in the pasta machine.

27

One time, someone eating in the dining room found a little pincher bug in her salad and said, "Waiter! There's a bug in my salad!" Tom whisked the salad away saying, "Oh, it must've fallen out of the flower arrangement. I'll get you another salad right away." Tom always made up stories. That little pincher bug didn't come from the flowers, it came from Bob's farm. It probably got stuck in the box when they picked the lettuce. How could anybody be afraid of a little pincher bug, anyway? They like lettuce as much as we do. It's like Bob says, "If the bugs like it, it must be good."

Bob's farm is up in Sonoma. He grows lettuce and vegetables and all kinds of things and sends them to the restaurant every day so they'll be fresh. Bob always tells my mom, "If you don't use the vegetables today, give them to somebody else who can, because vegetables have a certain life in them on the day they're picked, and if you don't eat them then and there they lose that life."

I always wondered what Bob meant. Life in vegetables? But he's right. It's like eating a peach you've just picked off a tree. It tastes so good. Beans, too. I used to hate beans, but now, every year in my backyard, we make a little teepee out of sticks and plant green beans at the bottom of each pole. The plants wind and climb up the poles and by the middle of the summer they make a little house that's just my size. It's a bean house and I can sit inside and pick and eat the sweetest beans and no one can see me.

Bob doesn't use sprays or poisons to kill the bugs and weeds at his farm. He's organic. Sometimes things get so overgrown that you can't tell where anything is planted. Bob always says, "Don't worry, when the vegetables come up, the weeds'll die down and you'll be able to see what to pick." Sometimes the bugs like the weeds better than the plants, anyway, and they leave the plants alone. Other times, like with snails, you have to go out in the garden yourself and gather them up by hand or they'll eat everything in sight. The best time to get snails is at night, because that's when they all like to come out the most. Sometimes my friends and I have flashlight parties. We all go out with our own flashlights and shine them on the snails. This really surprises them and they don't have time to get away. I think the owls in the trees think we're putting on some kind of weird light show for them but we're just trying to rid the garden of pests.

In July I help pick the flowers from the zucchini plants up at the farm. We use them to make stuffed squash blossoms. Bob always says, "Now pick as many blossoms as you can or else we're gonna be up to our ears in zucchini!" That's because every flower grows into a zucchini. Once the flowers are picked, we have to open the petals very carefully way down to the bottom and look inside to see if there are any bugs living there. Bugs or bees. I'm always afraid to look inside because you never know what might be there. One time, I opened up a stubborn blossom and a huge black beetle crawled out! Other times, though, you can open up the squash blossoms and find ladybugs or pretty caterpillar-like things. I always wish I'm going to find a little blue butterfly.

Every spring we all go up to Bob's farm to help him plant the potatoes and have a picnic. Everybody from the restaurant brings something they've made, and all the kids run around hiding in the bushes and eating little wild strawberries. People bring the weirdest things to eat: Brussels sprouts pizzas and hot chile peppers and one time my mom even made onion sandwiches. Can you believe that? Onion sandwiches? She just picked the spring onions from the ground and sliced them very, very thin and spread them on soft bread with a little mayonnaise and sprinkled them with salt and that was it. We dipped the sides in more mayonnaise and parsley and they were delish. My mom said it was a James Beard recipe, but I think she just made it up.

My mom says, "If you have good bread you can make a sandwich out of anything," and Steve says, "You can make good bread anywhere." Steve has his own bakery now, but when he was a busboy at the restaurant he taught himself to make bread right next to his bed at college. Steve would mix starters and doughs and bake them in all different ways in a little portable oven. Smoke and smells would come out of his dorm room and people all around the building would wonder what was going on. They must've thought it was a weird science project or something. Steve would bring samples of his bread into the restaurant and people would taste it and say things like, "Maybe you should bake it in a hotter oven." Or, "Why don't you spray the crust with water so it gets crispy?" Or, "Maybe you should use less yeast so it rises more slowly." Or, "Do you think it's too salty?" Finally, Steve brought in some really good bread and everyone stopped talking and just started eating.

Bumps makes special bread, too, and it takes all day to cook. Bumps is a friend of my mom's who has a boat up on the river, and at the end of every summer we go up there to swim. While Bumps's bread bakes in an iron pot in the middle of a barbecue, we go across the river to a place where fig trees grow. There's two kinds of figs that grow near Bumps's place: green figs that are white inside and purple figs that are red inside. I can never decide which ones I like the best. It's hard to find good ones because the birds always get there first. They know better than anybody which figs are the ripest and the sweetest and the best tasting. After we're done picking, we decorate a long table outside with all the figs and fig leaves, and then we all sit down next to the river and eat Bumps's bread while it's still warm. After dinner we cut up the figs and eat them for dessert. I always sneak away to feed some crumbs and scraps from the table to the carp. They're these fat old fish who live under the dock. The big carp swim up from the bottom, swallow a bunch of food, and then disappear back down into the black water. Bumps says some of the carp are over a hundred years old. I wonder if they've been eating crumbs for that long?

P.S. Bumps is not a real bump.

Carrie comes on Mondays and Fridays to make big bouquets all around the restaurant. She brings in giant stems of lilies and roses and buckets of water filled with tulips and dogwood and parts of bushes with kiwis and branches with apples or persimmons on them. She puts them all over the place and makes a big mess. The busboys are always trying to get the restaurant ready for the customers and the waiters are trying to set the tables and everybody's tripping over Carrie's branches and leaves and just trying to walk straight. Everyone worries that Carrie won't be able to finish making her arrangements by the time the restaurant opens but she always does and every time, just at the last minute, she starts up the vacuum and roars around and gets it all cleaned up just as the doors open. Sometimes the customers talk about the flowers more than the food.

I love it when the electricity goes out because we have to put candles all over the restaurant. It makes it kind of scary and fun. Of course, the dishwashing machines stop working, so nothing gets cleaned. The waiters start running out of plates and the busboys start running out of silverware and the cooks start running out of pots and the dishwashers start running out of room and my mom starts running out of patience. You can't even walk through the kitchen without knocking something over. Everybody who can goes down to the dish room to help out. They start twirling towels and spraying hoses and passing plates. My friend Zac always thinks it's a big waterfight and sprays everything with the big hose gun. With everybody helping we get most of the dishes done and, finally, the lights come on. Everybody goes back to their real jobs. Everyone, that is, except Zac. He pretends the waterfight is still on so he can spray me with that big hose gun.

There's this very nice lady who eats in the kitchen at least three times a week. Her name's Jean and we always thought she wanted to eat in the dining room but she said, "I don't care how busy it is, I always want to eat in the kitchen. That's where the food and my favorite people are." Jean always comes in a cab and brings me handmade chocolate candies made in a special shop in San Francisco. Once, for Halloween, she brought me this huge chocolate pumpkin that my mom made me share with all my friends at school. This other time, for Easter, though, Jean brought me a huge chocolate rabbit and I was going to eat that all by myself. But it melted.

I don't like wine very much, but my dad's always trying to get me to smell some. He tells me, "Pour the wine in a big, sparkling clean glass. Not too much. Now put your hands over both sides of the top and stick your nose down in between them. Now twirl the glass around a little and take a big sniff."

I always splash wine on my face or spill some on my hands. My dad gets very annoyed. Sometimes the wines smell like blackberries, sometimes they smell like currants or vanilla, sometimes they smell like tomatoes, but sometimes they smell just like wet leaves or like plain old dirt. I do like the smell of the wines that Lulu and Lucien make, but that's because I like Lulu and Lucien. The little boat on the label always reminds me of their house in France with all the bees and rosemary bushes and pine trees that look like umbrellas around it.

You have to be very careful when you're throwing things out at Chez Panisse because there are buckets all over the place, and every bucket is for a different kind of garbage. I always have to ask because it's very confusing. Some buckets are for all the paper garbage and some buckets are for bottles and some buckets are for the real garbage that goes in the dumpster and some are for the vegetable compost that goes back up to Bob's farm. I never want to take out our compost at home, but my mom says, "In six months those vegetable scraps will turn into rich, black dirt and we need that dirt for the garden. How else do you think things are going to grow?" She's right, you know. Vegetables take things out of the ground when they grow that you have to put back in or else vegetables won't grow there anymore.

Besides, it's an absolutely amazing thing. Magic.

You can put whole bananas and parts of oranges and stalks from

onions into the compost and they turn into black dirt. I layer the

vegetable scraps in our compost bin with layers of dirt and weeds.

I pretend I'm making this weird cake. Every six months or so I cut up the weird cake and spread it around the garden. I put the dirt near my favorite plants like the strawberry patch or the radishes or the mint plants. I can almost hear the plants saying, "Thank you" or "May I have seconds?"

I can never tell who actually runs Chez Panisse. I used to think it was my mom. She always said it was Tom because he always knew everything that was going on because he loved listening to what everybody had to say about everybody else. And then there's my grandpa—he's always talking to my mom on the phone about what she should do about money. And then there's Richard. Whenever there's a problem, someone says, "Richard—

> 1. The Toilet's broken!
> 2. The lights are out in the kitchen!
> 3. We need a piano upstairs!
> 4. Somebody's mad at so-and-so!
> 5. There's a crazy lady in the dining room!
>
> 6. WE NEED MORE MONEY!
> 7. The computer system totally doesn't work.

But, you know what? I don't even think Richard knows for sure who runs Chez Panisse.

P.S. I think Panisse runs Chez Panisse. He's up there on that poster in the café and, I think, at night when everyone's gone, he comes down with all his friends and they fix everything that's wrong.

When Chez Panisse turned twenty, they had their own outdoor farmers' market so everybody could meet all the people who grow food and raise animals for the restaurant. They closed Shattuck Avenue, and all the farmers set up booths with all kinds of fruits and vegetables and meats and cheeses, and even Carrie set up a booth with flowers. There were live trout in buckets, and one girl brought little lambs and put them in a little pen with hay. Another lady made tacos, patting out fresh tortillas with her hands, and Lindsey made her plum ice cream sandwiches and the Chinos let everybody taste all kinds of peppers. Paul roasted fresh almonds and Bob sold lettuce by the boxful and Niloufer cut up tropical fruit and put cayenne pepper on it and I even made little herb bouquets and sold them from a basket.

The street was really crowded with people who were looking at and smelling and tasting and buying all the wonderful food. Even Mama Cat came out of her alley to see what all the commotion was about. Everyone had a really good time, and all the farmers sold out of everything really quickly. My friends and I had the most fun because we sneaked under and around all the booths secretly tasting everything.

My favorite day at Chez Panisse is Bastille Day. Bastille Day is like the Fourth of July in France only it's on the fourteenth of July. There's a big party every year and everybody gets real French and kisses each other, and since Bastille Day happens at the same time of year that all the new garlic comes in, there's always a big, special garlic dinner that night. Everything they serve has garlic in it: garlic soup, garlic bread, roasted garlic, roasted chicken with garlic, garlic wine, garlic butter, garlic mayonnaise, garlic pizza, garlic oil, and one time they even had chocolate-covered garlic cloves. I'm not kidding.

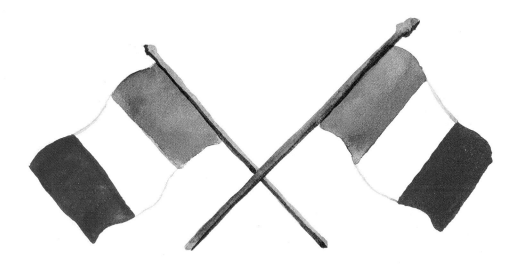

At the Bastille Day dinner there's music and laughing and every-body sits at long tables and talks to each other. The Head Garlic Lover wears a big hat that looks just like a big head of garlic—all billowy and white. He sits at a table like a king and presides over all the garlic eaters as they all try to see who can eat the most of the "stinking rose" (that's what they call garlic). People usually end up dancing all night.

My mom likes Bastille Day a lot because it makes her feel like she's in those old French movies she likes so much. Everyone gets together to eat and drink and laugh and talk and cry and sing and dance just like Fanny and Panisse and their friends did.

This year I finally got to go to the
Bastille Day Garlic Festival and I wore
my red-and-white striped tights and my blue skirt
and a French beret. Someone said I looked
like a little French flag.

Sometimes, after dinner, when all I want to do is go home and go to sleep, and my mom and all her friends are talking to each other and not paying any attention to me, I drift off and dream I'm in this other restaurant. This dream restaurant is in the middle of a garden and has just one big, long table where everybody sits and talks and eats with everybody else. There are big and little chairs for both kids and adults and Fritz is playing the piano and Michele is making pizzas and people are drawing all over the tablecloth. There are no waiters or waitresses—people just pick things from the garden and take them to the cooks and talk to the cooks while the cooks make their food. Everyone is eating with his hands, and dessert is served whenever you want it. All my friends are there, and we're eating corn on the cob and salad and tomatoes with aïoli and potatoes with aïoli and watermelon-lime juice and pizzas and green beans and garlic bread and warm tortillas with butter and passion fruits (my favorite) and little tangerines and strawberry ice on a stick and, just when I'm about to bite into a cherry tart, my mom wakes me up and says it's time to leave. So I always ask for just one chocolate kiss before we go home.

Restaurant

Recipes

I love to cook and these are some of my favorite recipes. Some of them I learned from my mom and my friends and from people in my family, and others I've just made up.

There are some very important things I've learned about safety in the kitchen that you should know, too, before you start to cook.

❧ Someone needs to help you—especially when you use the stove or oven.

❧ Knives are very sharp. I use little ones and I always cut away from my fingers. My mom always works with me when I'm cutting.

❧ Electrical appliances like the blender or mixer can be dangerous, so I always ask for help before turning these on.

My Mom's Special Rules

My mom is always saying these are the most important things she knows about food, so I wrote them down for her.

❧ Go to the market or garden *before* you decide what to cook.

❧ Taste, smell, touch, listen, and look carefully. All your senses tell you things about food: how to pick it, how to cook it, and how to eat it.

❧ Look for fruits and vegetables in season—those are always the ones that taste the best and cost the least.

❧ Always look for food that's organically grown. It is the healthiest for you, and organic farmers take care of the earth for all of us.

❧ Most of all, my mom says, "If you want to make people happy, cook them something good to eat."

Carrots,

Cucumbers,

and

Bell Peppers

Carrots and cucumbers and bell peppers are all vegetables that are good to eat raw. Carrots are roots, cucumbers grow on vines, and peppers grow on bushes. But they all come in different shapes and colors. Carrots aren't always orange; there are white and pink ones, too. Cucumbers aren't always long, skinny, and green; there are round, yellow ones called lemon cucumbers. And sweet bell peppers can be green, red, orange, yellow, purple, and brown!

CARROT AND PARSLEY SALAD

3 large carrots (½ pound)
⅓ cup chopped parsley (½ bunch)
½ small clove garlic
2 teaspoons red wine vinegar
2 tablespoons light olive oil or vegetable oil
Salt to taste, about ⅛ teaspoon

❧ Peel and wash the carrots. Use a grater to grate the carrots into fine threads. Use the small holes on the grater—not the large holes and not the finest ones you use for Parmesan cheese.

❧ Pick the leaves off a half bunch of parsley. Wash and dry the leaves, then chop them.

❧ Here is a neat trick for garlic: Peel a clove, then stand a fork up on its pointy ends in a bowl. Rub the garlic back and forth against the tips and it will make a juicy little puree of the garlic. In this way, puree half a clove. Add the vinegar and the oil and mix together.

❧ Stir in the carrots and parsley, season with salt, and mix very well. Sometimes I will eat this whole salad all by myself!

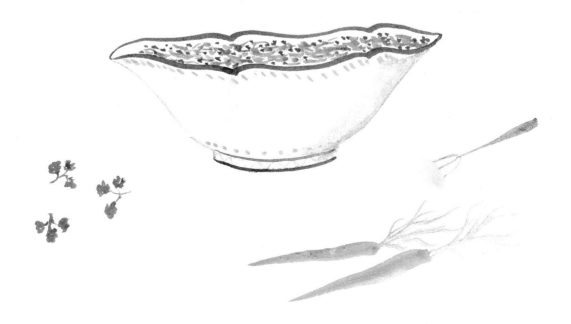

CUCUMBER RAITA

I first tasted this at our friend Niloufer's house. She comes from Bombay, India. She fried pooris (page 103)—crisp and puffy little wheat breads—and we dipped them in this sauce called raita. It's so good we use it as a sauce for almost everything at home—chicken, couscous, grilled fish, potatoes, and rice.

3 CUPS

1 medium-size cucumber (1 pound)
   (makes about 1 cup grated when water is squeezed out)
2 cups plain low-fat yogurt
1 small clove garlic
½ teaspoon salt

∾ Peel the cucumber with a vegetable peeler, and grate it using the large holes of a grater. One handful at a time, squeeze the water out of the grated cucumber (it's almost half water!).

∾ Put the cucumber into a bowl and mix with the yogurt, a small clove of garlic chopped fine, and salt. It's also good with chopped fresh coriander leaves (cilantro) added to it.

Roasted Peppers

These are great on pizza or pasta, in sandwiches, or just on a slice of toast for a snack.

~ Choose sweet, firm peppers of red, yellow, or other colors. Cut in half, and use a small knife to cut away the core at the top and the seeds inside.

~ Rub the skins on the outside with olive oil, and put the peppers skin-side up on a baking sheet. Bake them in a 375°F oven for 30 to 40 minutes until the skins are browned and blistery. Take them out of the oven and let them cool off.

~ Use your hands to pull off the browned skins. Cut the peppers into slices, and put in a bowl. Moisten with some olive oil and add a bit of salt. These will keep in the refrigerator, covered, for 5 or 6 days if you don't eat them right away.

Corn

I love corn. But I have to wait until July and August to eat it fresh on the cob. You can have cornbread and polenta all year round made out of cornmeal and corn flour. All these things are made with ground corn. Polenta is coarse ground, corn flour is fine ground, and cornmeal is in between. You can make corn flour by putting cornmeal or polenta in a spice grinder and whizzing it until it's the texture of flour. Lots of people think white corn is better than yellow corn, but what really matters is that fresh corn on the cob gets eaten just as soon as it gets picked. Then it will be really sweet.

CORNCAKES

My mom likes to eat these with caviar (fish eggs). I like to eat them with a berry syrup that I make by heating blueberries or strawberries with a little water and sugar until they are soft and juicy.

EIGHTEEN 2-INCH CAKES

1½ cups corn flour (not the kind called *masa harina*)
1½ teaspoons baking powder
½ teaspoon salt
2 eggs
1 tablespoon honey
1 cup milk
¼ cup vegetable oil or melted butter
1 ear sweet corn

∾ Mix the corn flour, baking powder, and salt together in a big bowl and make a well (a hole in the center) for the liquids.

∾ Separate the eggs and set the whites aside. In a small bowl, mix the egg yolk, honey, milk, and oil. Pour this into the well in the dry ingredients. Use a spoon to slowly mix the flour into the liquids. Stir it from the middle, gathering in the flour from the sides of the well, until it is all mixed together. Mixing this way helps prevent lumps and keeps the batter smooth.

∾ Beat the egg whites until they make soft peaks when you lift up the whisk or beater. Very gently fold the egg whites into the batter. Folding is different from stirring: Pour the egg whites on top of the batter and use a rubber spatula to lift up part of the batter from the bottom of the bowl and fold it over the egg whites. Do that again, turning the bowl a little after each time, until the whites are mostly mixed in. There are little air bubbles trapped in the beaten egg whites; if mixed too much or too hard they pop and go flat.

❧ Shuck the corn, and then cut the kernels off the cob. Hold it by the stalk, and stand it on end with the stalk at the top. Use a knife to cut straight down the side of the cob, slicing off the kernels. Stir the corn kernels into the batter.

❧ Cook on a lightly oiled medium-hot griddle or heavy frying pan. Turn them over as soon as bubbles form on the top.

CORNBREAD

¾ cup cornmeal
1 cup all-purpose flour
1 tablespoon sugar
1 tablespoon baking powder
¾ teaspoon salt
1 egg
1 cup milk
¼ cup melted butter

∾ Heat the oven to 425°F.

∾ Mix the cornmeal, flour, sugar, baking powder, and salt in a bowl. Make a well (a hole) in the middle and add the egg and milk. Gently stir the dry things into the milk and egg until it is all mixed and smooth. Stir in the melted butter.

∾ Pour the batter into a buttered 8-inch or 9-inch pie pan or cast-iron pan and bake about 20 minutes until browned on top.

POLENTA

Polenta is the Italian word for cornmeal cooked in water. We eat it freshly cooked, when it's soft and creamy, with pasta sauce. Or we let it cool until it gets firm, cut it in pieces, and bake, fry, or grill it.

4 SERVINGS

2 cups water
½ teaspoon salt
½ cup polenta

❧ Heat the water to boiling in a heavy-bottomed pot. Lower the heat so it is gently bubbling, and add the salt.

❧ While stirring all the time, slowly pour the polenta into the water. Keep stirring for about 5 minutes until evenly thickened and soupy. Adjust the heat so it just barely bubbles, and cook another 15 minutes, stirring every few minutes to keep it from sticking to the bottom. If it gets thicker than you like, just add water in small amounts until it is the texture you want.

❧ When it is done you can eat it right away while it is soft—it is delicious this way with butter and Parmesan cheese—or you can pour it onto an oiled pan and let it get cool and firm. Then it can be cut into pieces and baked, fried, or grilled and served with cheese, sauce, vegetables, mushrooms, or whatever.

QUESADILLAS

I love to eat these when I come home from school in the afternoon.

8 QUESADILLAS

> 12 ounces Monterey Jack cheese
> 16 corn tortillas
> 1 cup tomato salsa (page 93)
> Optional: chopped hot chile peppers or sweet red peppers;
>   cilantro leaves

❧ First grate the cheese. Put a lightly oiled cast-iron pan or griddle on the stove over medium heat.

❧ Lay out 8 of the tortillas on the table and spread cheese over each one. Spoon some salsa on the cheese and top with the rest of the tortillas—like making sandwiches. If you like, add chile peppers and cilantro.

❧ Use a spatula and slip the tortilla sandwich into the hot pan. Cook for 2 to 3 minutes, then turn over and cook another minute or so until the cheese is melted. Remove with the spatula, cut into quarters, and eat right away.

If we have leftover tortillas, sometimes my mom cuts them in strips and shallow-fries them in hot oil to make fresh corn chips.

Thyme

Chives

Rosemary

Basil

Bay Laurel

Herbs

Fresh herbs are magic, like flowers. Herbs are my favorite part of cooking. You can change the flavor and smell of something just by changing the herb. Basil is one of my favorites. You can pound it with garlic to make a pesto sauce for pasta. I make my own flavors of herb tea with lemon thyme and mint. I love borage, too. The bright blue flowers taste like cucumbers.

TISANE

Tisane is a French word for a kind of hot tea. You make it by soaking fresh herbs in very hot water. In English it is called an infusion because the herbs *infuse* the water with flavor. There are lots of different kinds. Here are some of the ones we make: lemon verbena; lemon balm; chamomile; mint of all kinds; thyme, lemon thyme, lime thyme; citronella; rosemary; rose hips, buds, and petals; orange blossoms; and chrysanthemum buds. Make sure the herbs are organic so you know they don't have chemical sprays on them.

> 2 to 3 cups boiling water
> Handful of fresh tisane herbs

∾ Warm the teapot with hot water to begin. Pour out that water, then put the herbs in the pot. Pour the boiling water over the herbs and allow to steep for 4 to 5 minutes. Drink from small beautiful cups, refilling often, with or without the addition of honey.

Gremolata

This is a mixture of fresh parsley, garlic, and lemon rind that tastes really good on just about anything: grilled chicken or fish, stews and pastas, even on scrambled eggs.

> 1 small bunch parsley
> 1 lemon
> 1 clove garlic

∾ Wash and dry the parsley. Pull the leaves off the stems and chop fine. Grate just the yellow rind of the lemon using the finest holes of a grater. Peel and chop the garlic very fine. Mix the three together in a small bowl. Sprinkle on grilled chicken, or whatever you like, right after cooking and before serving.

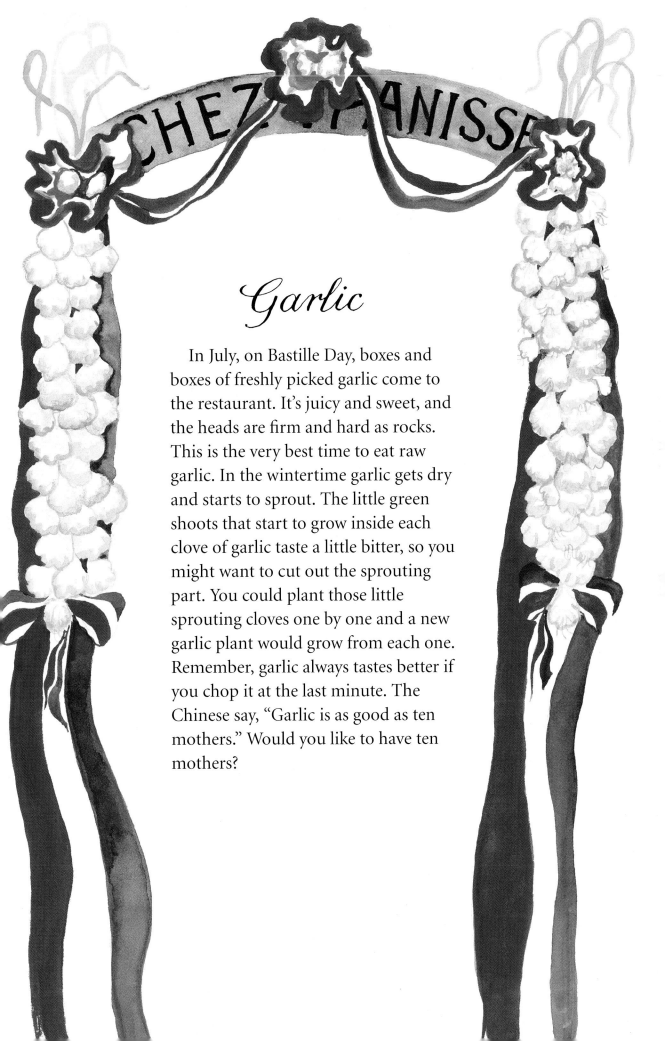

Garlic

In July, on Bastille Day, boxes and boxes of freshly picked garlic come to the restaurant. It's juicy and sweet, and the heads are firm and hard as rocks. This is the very best time to eat raw garlic. In the wintertime garlic gets dry and starts to sprout. The little green shoots that start to grow inside each clove of garlic taste a little bitter, so you might want to cut out the sprouting part. You could plant those little sprouting cloves one by one and a new garlic plant would grow from each one. Remember, garlic always tastes better if you chop it at the last minute. The Chinese say, "Garlic is as good as ten mothers." Would you like to have ten mothers?

Pasta with Garlic and Parsley

This is what we eat when we come home from a trip and everyone is very tired and hungry right now.

2 SERVINGS

> 4 ounces linguine, spaghettini, or other pasta
> 3 small cloves (or more) garlic
> 3 to 4 tablespoons chopped parsley
> 4 tablespoons olive oil
> Salt and pepper

❧ Put a large pot of water on the stove to boil.

❧ Peel and chop the garlic, and chop the parsley.

❧ When the water is boiling, add some salt and put in the pasta. When it is nearly cooked, heat the olive oil in a large sauté pan and very gently cook the garlic so it just sizzles. Be careful not to let it brown.

❧ Drain the pasta. Take the sauté pan off the heat and add the pasta. Mix it all together; add the parsley, some salt and pepper, and mix again.

It's good just like that but sometimes we add things like Parmesan cheese, rocket (arugula) or basil instead of parsley, chopped anchovies or olives, fresh tomatoes, and pine nuts or walnuts.

GARLIC CROUTONS

Croutons are pieces of bread toasted with olive oil. You can eat them whole with roasted peppers, tomatoes, or anything else you like on top, or you can break the croutons up into bite-size pieces and add to a salad.

❧ Cut slices of good tasty bread and brush or rub olive oil all over one side. Toast the slices on a baking sheet in a hot oven until lightly browned. (My mom likes to grill the bread over a low fire.) Remove from the oven and while still warm, rub all over the oiled side with a clove of raw garlic.

Garlic Mayonnaise (Aïoli)

Aïoli is the word for garlic mayonnaise in Provence, in the south of France. In the summer we make platters of grilled fish, green beans, potatoes, eggs, peppers, tomatoes, and croutons and pass around a big bowl of aïoli. You can make plain mayonnaise if you want to. Just leave out the garlic.

1¼ CUPS

> 1 egg at room temperature
> Salt
> 1 cup light olive oil or vegetable oil
> ½ clove garlic
> Vinegar or lemon juice
> Pepper

∾ Separate the egg and put the yolk in a medium-size bowl. Season with a good pinch of salt. It is important that the egg be at room temperature or a little warmer. The egg and oil won't mix well if the egg is cold. Set the bowl on a damp dish towel so it won't slip and slide while you're mixing.

∾ Measure 1 cup oil into a container with a pour spout. Mix the egg and salt together with a whisk. Whisking all the time, slowly add the oil to the egg *drop by drop*. It will thicken gradually as the egg absorbs the oil. If too much oil is added at once, the egg and oil will separate and won't go back together. So it is important to be patient at the beginning—later, when it gets thick, you can add more oil at once.

∾ It will start to get quite thick after you have mixed in about ¼ cup oil. Thin it by adding ½ teaspoon warm water, then continue to add the oil in a thin, steady stream. It will be quite thick again after you have mixed in about ¾ cup oil. Thin again with ½ teaspoon warm water, and whisk in the remaining oil in a steady stream.

∾ Make a puree of the garlic. Pound it in a mortar with a pestle until smooth and juicy—this is fun. Or rub the clove against the pointy ends of a fork held against the bottom of a bowl. Add about half the puree to the mayonnaise. It's better to start with a little garlic because you can always add more to make it taste stronger, but you can't take some out later if it is too garlicky.

∾ Finish the seasoning by adding about ¼ teaspoon of white or red wine vinegar or lemon juice and a pinch of salt and pepper. Taste and add more vinegar or salt if needed. Is the garlic flavor strong enough? Add a bit more puree if you like. Keep chilled in the refrigerator if you're not going to eat it right away. It is best if eaten the same day it is made, but will keep 2 to 3 days in the refrigerator.

Lettuce Salad

I like salad with lots of different kinds of lettuces. We eat them every day and the mixture changes all year round depending on what's growing. You've got to be careful when you choose lettuce. Small lettuces are more tender than large overgrown ones. Fresh lettuce looks like it's still growing.

LETTUCE GREENS

❧ To prepare the lettuces: Remove any damaged leaves on the outside. Separate the heads into individual leaves. Tear large leaves into smaller pieces. Wash them gently in a bowl in plenty of cold water. Lift the lettuces out and drain.

❧ Spin dry in a salad spinner or lettuce dryer. Only fill it half full at a time. The most important thing is to have dry lettuce or the dressing won't coat the leaves. As they are dried, spread them out on a towel. Roll the towel up loosely, put in an airtight bag, and refrigerate until ready to serve.

❧ Toss the salad in vinaigrette dressing just before serving.

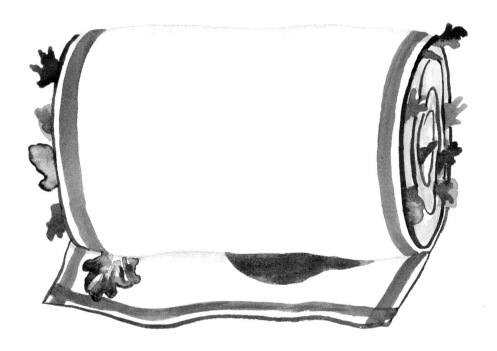

Vinaigrette

Vinaigrette is the French word for oil and vinegar dressing. At the restaurant they have an olive oil tasting every year to decide which kinds to buy, because each year's crop of olives tastes a little different. Olive oils come from Spain, France, Greece, Italy, Mexico, and California. The dark green "extra virgin" oils taste the most like olives. The cooks use extra virgin olive oil for salad dressing, not to cook with. The paler, yellow oils labeled "pure olive oil" taste milder, and those get used for cooking.

> 1 shallot (optional)
> Salt
> 2 tablespoons red wine vinegar
> 5 to 6 tablespoons extra virgin olive oil

∾ Peel the shallot and cut into very thin slices. Put in a small bowl with a pinch of salt and the vinegar. Let the shallot soak in the vinegar for 15 to 20 minutes, then stir in the olive oil and mix well. Taste to see if the balance of the vinegar and oil is right—you might need to add more of one or the other. This is enough for 4 generous servings of salad.

Fruit

In the summertime, it seems like every dessert at Chez Panisse is either peaches or apricots or cherries. There aren't any recipes for cherries here, because I always eat them all up first.

In August, the apples on my tree are ripe so we always make lots of applesauce for my birthday. Usually it's hard to find more than a few kinds of apples at the store, but at the farmers' market in the fall there are lots of them. My mom always says, "Look for the ones that are organically grown! They're the best ones."

Berries don't get ripe after you pick them, so if they are very tart when you buy them they will need lots of sugar to make them sweet. But the more sugar you add, the less berry flavor you have. To find the sweetest, ripest berries, you have to wait until the summer.

PEACH CRISP

You can make a crisp with many other fruits—apples, nectarines, apricots—and you can mix berries in with them, too. It's also very good with half a cup of nuts cut in small pieces and added to the topping.

6 TO 8 SERVINGS

CRISP TOPPING:

1 cup flour

⅓ cup brown sugar

1 tablespoon granulated sugar

⅓ cup butter (about ¾ stick) at room temperature

4 pounds ripe, firm peaches

1 ½ tablespoons flour

1 tablespoon sugar

∾ To make the topping, mix the flour and sugars in a bowl. Cut the butter into small pieces and add to the bowl. Mix in the butter by rubbing it in the flour mixture lightly and quickly between your fingertips. When the butter, flour, and sugar are evenly mixed and the mixture looks crumbly, it's ready.

∾ Cut the peaches in half, peel, and remove the pits. Cut into slices. There should be about 8 cups. Mix them with the flour and sugar. If the peaches are sweet you won't need any sugar. If using other fruits, taste to decide how much sugar to add.

∾ Spread the peaches in a 2-quart glass or ceramic ovenproof dish, and sprinkle the topping evenly over the peaches. Bake in a preheated 375°F oven for about 40 minutes, until the topping is brown and the peaches are thick and bubbly. It is nice to eat warm, after it has cooled a bit, with some fresh cream poured around it on the dish.

APRICOT JAM

2½ to 3 pounds ripe, sweet apricots
3 cups sugar
¼ cup water
Juice of 1 lemon

∾ Wash the apricots, cut in half, and remove the pits. Cut each half into 2 or 3 pieces. Put in a heavy stainless steel pan, add the sugar and water, stir, and let sit for 30 to 60 minutes (or overnight) to let the sugar dissolve and draw out the apricot juices.

∾ Heat the apricots to boiling over medium heat, stirring now and then. When it first begins to boil, a light foam will form on the top. Use a spoon to skim off the foam. Boil the apricots gently, stirring occasionally, for 15 to 20 minutes until thick.

∾ Test to see if it is thick enough this way: Put a small plate in the freezer so it is very cold. Remove it and put a small spoonful of jam on the plate. This will cool it right away and you can judge what consistency it will be when cool. If not thick enough, put the plate back in the freezer, cook the jam another few minutes, and test again.

∾ Add the lemon juice at the very end. Lemon juice helps balance the sweetness, and also has natural pectin that will help thicken the jam. Turn off the heat, let cool a bit, and then carefully ladle the jam into warm, sterile jars. (To sterilize jars, wash them in soapy water, rinse them, and put them in a large pot. Cover them with water and bring slowly to a boil. Remove the jars carefully with tongs and fill them right away, while they're still warm.) Cover until cooled, and put 2 thin layers of melted paraffin (household wax) on the jam and seal the jars with tight covers.

BLACKBERRY ICE CREAM

Make sure you pick enough blackberries. I usually eat half of them before they get in the bucket.

1 QUART

> 2 to 3 cups ripe blackberries (to make 1 cup puree)
> 4 egg yolks
> 1 cup sugar
> 1 cup milk
> 2 to 3 drops vanilla extract, to taste
> 1 cup whipping cream

∾ First puree the berries and then strain out the seeds to make 1 cup puree. A food mill works better than a blender because it won't break up the seeds, which taste bitter.

∾ Then make the custard (it's called *crème anglaise* in French): Mix the egg yolks with the sugar in a medium-size bowl. Heat the milk until hot but not boiling, and stir it slowly into the egg yolks and sugar.

∾ Put it back on the stove and heat it gently, stirring all the time, until it just thickens. You'll know it's ready when you lift the spoon out and draw your finger through the custard on it; if it coats the spoon, and you can draw a clear line through it, it's done. You can also check it with a thermometer: When it reaches 170°F, it's ready. *Right away* pour it through a strainer into a bowl. Stir in the vanilla and then put the custard in the refrigerator to get cold.

∾ When the custard is cold, add the cream and blackberry puree and it's ready to go into the ice-cream freezer. Follow the directions for your particular freezer.

The vanilla custard with the cream added at the end, without the berry puree, is how you make vanilla ice cream. So just skip the berries and freeze it, and you have vanilla ice cream.

You can also add a puree of some other kind of berry or juicy fruit to make different kinds of ice cream from this vanilla base.

GOLDEN DELICIOUS APPLESAUCE

Tasty apples will make sweet applesauce without any sugar at all. Sometimes the apples are too sweet and you need to add a little lemon juice.

2 CUPS

1 pound apples
¼ cup water

❧ Cut the apples into quarters. Use a small knife (a paring knife) to cut off the peels and remove the cores, and cut into chunks.

❧ Put the apple chunks in a saucepan with ¼ cup water on the stove over medium heat. Heat to a gentle simmer, then cover and cook for 20 to 30 minutes until soft.

❧ Stir every once in a while during the cooking, and when soft, mash with a spoon to the texture you like. Try it warm with crème fraîche.

Potatoes

Potatoes grow underground while no one is watching. Besides red and white potatoes and the big dusty looking ones called russets that people usually bake, there are purple ones and long yellow ones that look like knobby fingers (called fingerlings).

Roast Potatoes and Garlic Mayonnaise

Potatoes are especially good in the early summer, pulled up when they are young and small. Little new potatoes are delicious roasted in their skins. Some different kinds are Yellow Finnish, Rose Fir, and Fingerling.

4 SERVINGS

20 to 24 small new potatoes
1½ tablespoons olive oil
Salt and pepper
2 or 3 sprigs each thyme and rosemary
2 bay leaves
1 recipe Garlic Mayonnaise (page 74)

ꙮ Wash the potatoes and leave the skins on. If they're small, don't cut them, otherwise cut in half or quarters. Put them in an earthenware or ceramic ovenproof dish. Pour over the olive oil, and season with salt and pepper. Add the herbs to the dish and stir the potatoes so they are coated with oil.

ꙮ Bake in a 350° to 375°F oven, stirring every so often, until tender and browned, about 50 to 60 minutes. The potatoes are very good dipped in garlic mayonnaise just by themselves, or alongside grilled or baked fish.

Sometimes in the summer we have a dinner of vegetables—potatoes, green beans, peppers, and tomatoes, with garlic mayonnaise, a salad, and croutons, and it's the best.

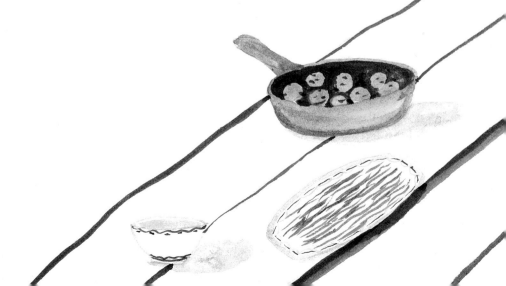

Tomatoes

Tomatoes come in all colors and shapes. There is even a tomato called "Green Grape" that looks just like one. My mom never buys tomatoes all winter long no matter how good they look. July, August, and September are the tomato months because they are the only months when the sun is hot enough to ripen the fruit on the plant. The special sweetness of a summer tomato must be the reason the French gave them the name *pommes d'amour*, which means "love apples."

TOMATO SALAD

A mixture of different kinds and colors of tomatoes makes a great salad. It's not just the colors and shapes that are different, but they have their own flavors too. Some are sweet, some are tart, and some are both. Some are very juicy and some are firm. Any combination works as long as the tomatoes are ripe and tasty. I also love to put in big chunks of garlic croutons to soak up all the juices.

4 SERVINGS

> 1 pound ripe tomatoes: Early Girls, Sweet 100's,
>   Golden Jubilees, red and yellow cherry tomatoes
> ½ clove garlic
> 1 tablespoon balsamic or red wine vinegar
> 2 to 3 tablespoons olive oil
> Salt and pepper
> 2 ounces mozzarella cheese
> Handful fresh basil leaves

∾ Wash the tomatoes, cut out the core at the top, and cut into thick slices or wedges. Cut cherry tomatoes in half.

∾ Peel the garlic and in the bottom of a bowl or platter, rub it against the pointy tips of a fork to make a puree. Mix the vinegar and oil with the garlic. Add the tomatoes and use your hands to gently toss the tomatoes in the dressing. Season with salt and pepper.

∾ Slice the mozzarella and tuck it in and around the tomatoes. Scatter the basil leaves over the top.

CHERRY TOMATO PASTA

4 SERVINGS

2 baskets cherry tomatoes (about 5 cups)
1 cup extra virgin olive oil
1 tablespoon red wine vinegar
Fresh basil or parsley
Salt and pepper
¾ to 1 pound dry linguine
Optional: 1½ cups fresh bread crumbs

❧ While a big pot of water heats to boiling, prepare the tomatoes. Slice the tomatoes in half. Put them in a big bowl and add the olive oil and vinegar. Chop some fresh basil and or parsley and add to the tomatoes. Season with salt and pepper. Stir and let it all sit for a while.

❧ Cook the noodles and drain them, then add to the bowl of tomatoes. Mix well and serve onto plates, spooning the tomatoes and juices over the noodles.

❧ Crunchy bread crumbs are very good added at the very end. Toast the fresh bread crumbs (page 107) on a cookie sheet in the oven until browned. Toss with a little olive oil, and mix into the noodles after the tomatoes.

Tomato Sauce

3 pounds ripe, sweet tomatoes (14 to 16 medium size)
1 medium carrot
1 medium onion
1 small stalk celery
¼ cup olive oil
1 sprig thyme
1 bay leaf
2 large cloves garlic, chopped
1 teaspoon salt

∿ Wash the tomatoes, remove the core at the top, and cut each into 8 or more wedges.

∿ Prepare the mixture of carrot, onion, and celery. In French this is called *mirepoix*; the cooks use it to flavor broths, sauces, stews, fish, pasta, and more. Peel the carrot and onion, then cut or chop each vegetable into small pieces.

∿ Heat a saucepan of at least 2 quarts over medium heat. Add the olive oil, chopped vegetables, thyme, and bay leaf. Cover the mirepoix and cook gently for 10 minutes until the vegetables soften—they should not brown. Add the garlic and cook another minute, then add the tomatoes and salt.

∿ Cover and cook for 20 minutes, stirring from time to time, until the tomatoes are very juicy. Remove the cover and cook another 15 to 20 minutes. Taste the sauce; you may want to adjust the flavor with a bit of sugar or vinegar. Put the sauce through a food mill to puree all the vegetables and strain out the seeds and skin. The sauce will likely be a good texture for pasta, but you might want to cook it down to a thicker texture to use on pizza.

Tomato Salsa

I like to make a lot of salsa—for guacamole, quesadillas, and enough for my dad to eat with chips.

2½ CUPS

    6 ripe tomatoes, to make 2 cups chopped
    ½ small onion
    ½ bunch cilantro
    1 large or 2 small cloves garlic
    ½ teaspoon salt
    Juice of ½ lime

∾ Wash and core the tomatoes (cut out the end where the stem is attached to the tomato). Then slice them and cut them again into little squares. Peel and cut the onion the same way.

∾ Pick the leaves off the cilantro branches and chop the cilantro very fine so that it makes about 3 tablespoons. Peel and chop the garlic fine. Stir it all together with the salt and lime juice.

∾ Taste it. Does it need a little more salt or lime juice? It tastes better after it sits for about 15 minutes. My dad likes to add some chopped hot chiles, but I only let him put in a little because I don't like it too spicy.

GUACAMOLE

This is really fun to make because you just mash up avocados. You can make it as spicy or as plain as you want.

1 large, ripe avocado
Juice of ½ lime
½ cup tomato salsa (page 93)
¼ to ½ teaspoon salt

❧ Peel the avocado and remove the pit. Put the avocado in a bowl and mash it with a fork. Add the lime juice, salsa, and salt and mix it all together. Taste to see if it needs more salt or lime juice.

Bread and Pizza

Any bread you make yourself and eat fresh is just
great. You can make good bread from flour, water,
yeast, and salt. Some breads—like tortillas and Indian
pooris—don't even need yeast to make them rise. But it
takes time to make bread, and maybe that's why it's
hard to get good bread. I guess people won't take
enough time to make it, or they wait too long to eat it
after it's baked. If you bake bread at home, it will warm
your whole house.

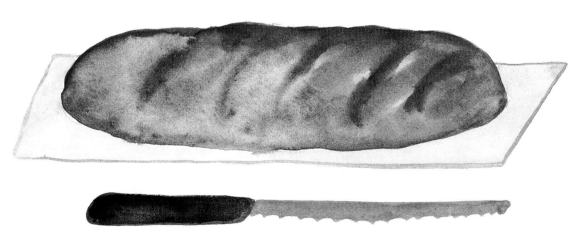

WHITE AND WHOLE WHEAT BREAD

1 package (¼ ounce) dry yeast
¼ cup warm water
3 cups all-purpose flour
½ cup whole wheat flour
½ cup warm water
½ cup milk
2 teaspoons salt
2 tablespoons olive oil

❧ Dissolve the yeast in ¼ cup warm water, about the same temperature as your body.

❧ Measure the flours into a large bowl and make a well (a hole) in the center. Pour in the yeast and water, and use a big wooden spoon to mix into the flour. Then make a well in the center again.

❧ Mix the warm water and milk together, and stir in the salt. Pour that into the well along with the olive oil. Mix with a spoon and then your hands until it gets thick and starts to come together, forming a shaggy ball.

❧ Take the dough out of the bowl and knead it on a lightly floured table—use the heel of your hand and push down on the dough. Fold it in half, turn it around a bit, and push down again. Repeat the pushing, folding, and turning movements over and over for 2 minutes.

❧ Clean the bowl and rub oil on the inside. Put the dough in the bowl and roll it around so it is oiled all over. Cover the bowl with a damp towel and set in a warm place to rise. (Inside the oven with just the warmth of the pilot light is a good place.) It should rise until double in size, about 45 minutes.

↶ Take the dough out of the bowl and knead on the table. Knead it *hard* this time, for 5 minutes.

↶ Oil a bread pan. Shape the bread by pressing it out flat, then roll it tightly to make a cylinder about as long as the bread pan. Tuck the ends under to make them a bit square, and put in the pan with the seam on the bottom. Lightly oil the top and sprinkle with a little flour—this is just for looks.

↶ Cover the pan with the towel, and let rise again. It should rise about 45 to 60 minutes. Remove the towel near the end of the rising. Take the bread out of the oven if it is rising there, and turn the oven on to 425°F. You can test to see if it has risen enough by gently pressing a fingertip into the dough. If it doesn't spring back and the shape of your fingertip remains, it is ready.

↶ Bake at 425°F for 15 minutes, then turn the oven down to 400°F and bake another 30 minutes. Baking it hot makes a nice crust. The traditional way to test to see if it is done is to tap the loaf with your finger, and if it sounds hard and hollow it is done. If it makes a soft and dull sound, bake another 5 minutes and test again. Let the bread cool on a rack so it doesn't steam in the pan and soften the crust.

To make bread with more whole wheat flavor just change the flour proportions to 2 cups all-purpose and 1½ cups whole wheat.

If you want to interrupt the process and refrigerate the dough, the best time to do it is after the dough is shaped and in the pan. Cover it well before refrigerating. When you take it out it will take a half hour or more to come to room temperature and then begin to rise.

Pizza Dough

¾ cup warm water

1 tablespoon milk

2 teaspoons active dry yeast

2 cups all-purpose flour

½ teaspoon salt

2 tablespoons olive oil

Extra flour and olive oil

❧ Measure the water and milk into a big bowl. Add the yeast and stir with a wooden spoon. Stir in the flour, salt, and olive oil. Mix it all together with the spoon until it is too thick and sticky to stir.

❧ Spread a little flour on a kitchen table and put the dough on the table. Knead it with your hands by gathering dough from the sides and folding it to the middle. Do that over and over, turning it around now and then, until the dough becomes smooth. If it sticks to the table or your hands, add a little more flour.

❧ Clean and dry the bowl. Rub the bottom and sides with olive oil and put the dough into the bowl. Cover the bowl with a towel and put it in a warm place. Let the dough rise about 1½ hours.

❧ Then it needs to be punched down with a fist in the middle of the dough. This will let the air out so it can rise again. Turn it over to make it into a ball, cover the bowl again, and let it rise another hour.

❧ Heat the oven to 450°F. Roll out the dough with a rolling pin, or use your hands to pat it out into a circle about 12 to 14 inches across and about ⅛ to ¼ inch thick. Put it on an oiled baking sheet and top with what you like: grated mozzarella and Parmesan cheese, olive oil and garlic, slices of tomatoes or tomato sauce.

☙ Bake about 15 minutes until browned and crisp. A little parsley or basil sprinkled on after it is baked is very good.

How to Bake Pizza

☙ Bake pizza in a very hot oven, 450°F, so the crust will be both crisp and nicely browned. You can bake the pizza directly on unglazed ceramic tiles in your oven; this makes for a very crisp texture on the bottom crust. Put the tiles, or a baking stone, on a rack in the oven before heating it. After you flatten out the dough to form the pizza, spread some flour on the back of a baking sheet and lay the dough on it. Put the toppings on the pizza, and when it is ready to bake, slide it off the baking sheet onto the tiles.

You can also bake it on a lightly oiled pizza pan or baking sheet. Roll out the dough with a rolling pin, or press it out with your hands so it is ⅛ to ¼ inch thick, then transfer it to the baking sheet. Make it a little thicker at the edges for a good crust. It will bake in about 15 minutes.

Tomato Sauce and Mozzarella Cheese Pizza

∾ Roll out the dough, and spread about ¾ cup of thick tomato sauce (page 92) over the top. Put about 4 to 6 ounces grated mozzarella cheese and a light grating of Parmesan cheese on the tomato sauce and bake. Add fresh chopped herbs, such as basil and parsley, when it comes out of the oven.

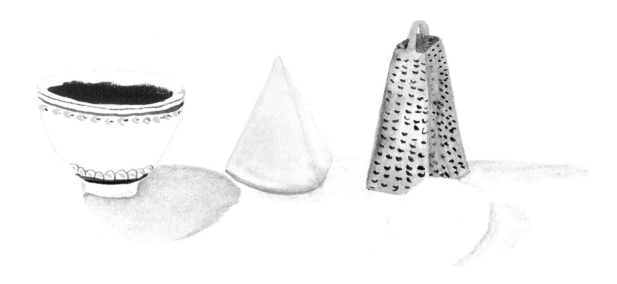

Colored Peppers Pizza

∾ Cut 3 bell peppers of different colors—red, yellow, and green—into slices. Roll out the dough, and spread a light layer of chopped garlic and olive oil on the dough. Then put about 4 ounces of grated mozzarella cheese all over it. Put the pepper slices on top of the cheese, and bake. When it is done, dribble a little olive oil around the edges, and sprinkle with chopped parsley.

CALZONE

Calzone is a big turnover pizza—half the flattened dough is folded over the filling and the edges are sealed together.

> 4 ounces goat cheese
> 7 ounces mozzarella cheese
> 2 thin slices prosciutto
> 2 tablespoons fresh chives
> 2 tablespoons parsley
> 1 sprig each fresh thyme and marjoram
> 2 small cloves garlic
> Black pepper
> 1 recipe pizza dough (page 98)

∾ Crumble the goat cheese and grate the mozzarella. Cut the prosciutto into matchstick-size pieces. Slice the chives and chop the parsley fine. Remove the leaves from the sprigs of thyme and marjoram and chop fine. Peel and chop the garlic cloves. Mix everything together in a bowl and add a pinch of black pepper.

∾ Roll the pizza dough into a circle about 14 inches across. Put the cheese filling on half of the dough circle, leaving a little space at the edges. Moisten the edges next to the cheese with a little water. Fold the other half of the dough over the filling to make the edges meet. Start at one end and fold the dough up onto itself, pressing and pinching each fold down and closed as you move around to the other end.

∾ Lift onto a lightly oiled baking sheet or slide onto baking tiles in the oven, and bake about 20 minutes until brown and crisp. When you take it from the oven, brush with olive oil and serve right away.

BISCUITS

This is so easy my mom lets me make biscuits all by myself. I like to eat them when they are hot with some butter and jam, or make strawberry shortcake with them.

TWELVE TO FIFTEEN 2-INCH BISCUITS

1¾ cups flour
1 tablespoon baking powder
1 tablespoon sugar
½ teaspoon salt
1 cup whipping cream
2 to 3 tablespoons melted butter

∾ First turn the oven on to 425°F. Then put all the dry things—flour, baking powder, sugar, and salt—into a medium-size bowl, and mix with a spoon. Pour in the cream and mix with a spoon until it forms big lumps. Then mix with your hands. At first it is sticky, but as you press it together it begins to form a smooth ball.

∾ Take the ball out of the bowl and put it on a lightly floured table. Press the dough out with your hands, fold it back onto itself, and press out again. Turn it around and press and fold again. This is called "kneading" the dough. Do it for about 1 minute.

∾ Roll out the dough with a rolling pin, or use your hand to pat it out. It should be about ¾ inch thick—about two fingers high. Cut into shapes you like with a cookie cutter or an upside-down glass. This makes about 12 round biscuits, but you have to roll the scraps of dough together again to make the last ones.

∾ Have a baking sheet ready. Dip each biscuit in the melted butter. Let the extra butter drip off, and then put the biscuit on the sheet. Bake them for 12 to 15 minutes until nice and brown.

POORIS

A poori is like a freshly made tortilla with a toasty whole wheat flavor. They are shallow-fried and puff up like balloons in the hot oil. I make the dough and roll it out and my mom does the frying because that's the hard part. I love to eat them with cucumber raita and chicken.

12 POORIS

4 ounces whole wheat flour
4 ounces all-purpose flour
½ teaspoon salt
2 tablespoons vegetable oil
½ cup water
Oil for frying

∾ Mix the flours and salt together in a bowl. Sprinkle the oil onto the flour. Mix with your fingertips. Add the water and use your hands to mix and gather it into a ball of dough.

∾ Take the dough out of the bowl and knead it on the table, pushing it down and folding it over. Do it as long as you can—about 10 minutes—until it is very smooth. Wrap it in plastic, and let it rest 30 minutes.

∾ Divide the dough into 12 pieces and roll into balls. Wrap again, and let rest 15 minutes more.

∾ Heat a cast-iron pan filled 1 inch deep with vegetable oil until the oil is quite hot (375°F). Roll out the balls of dough into circles about 5 inches across. They will be very thin. Fry one at a time. They will puff up quickly in the hot oil; turn them over and cook on the other side. Lift out of the oil with a strainer and drain on paper towels. Eat right away while still warm.

Fish

Really fresh fish doesn't smell fishy and it sparkles and glistens. My mom talks to Paul, the man who sells her fish, and asks him what came in today. Then she buys that one because she says it's always the best. The fish you *know* are fresh are the live ones. Sometimes I see crabs and lobster and catfish at the market alive in tanks, and then I know they'll taste good.

Halibut Baked on a Fig Leaf

The fig leaves are not really for eating. They keep the fish juicy while it cooks and make it smell like coconut. You can cook these in the oven or on a grill.

4 SERVINGS

4 large fig leaves
4 halibut fillets, ½ to 1 inch thick
4 tablespoons olive oil
Salt and pepper
Lemon

∾ Heat the oven to 375°F. Wash the fig leaves, and put them on the table, shiny side up. Put the fish in the middle of each leaf. Oil the fish on both sides, and sprinkle with salt and pepper.

∾ Fold up the fig leaf over the fish to make a package. Put the folded side down when you place it on a baking sheet or on the grill so that it will stay closed. If you're baking the fish, pour about ¼ cup water on the baking sheet.

∾ Put the baking sheet with the four packages in the oven for about 10 minutes. (If grilling the fish, cook 3 to 4 minutes on one side, then turn it over and cook another 3 to 4 minutes.) To see if it is done, open up one of the packages and look at the center of the fish. If it is white and flaky all through, it's done. Remember, it will continue to cook a bit after you take it from the oven, so don't cook it too much. Put the packages on plates, and let each person open their own. It is good with a squeeze of lemon and a little extra salt.

LEMON SOLE FRIED WITH BREAD CRUMBS

This is fun to make. You get to dip the fish in flour, egg, and bread crumbs. The flour makes the egg stick, and the egg makes the bread crumbs stick, and everything sticks to your fingers. This way of cooking fish is great for chicken breast fillets, too.

4 SERVINGS

2 eggs
½ cup flour
½ teaspoon salt
¼ teaspoon pepper
2 to 2½ cups fresh bread crumbs (page 107)
4 fillets of lemon sole or other thin, delicate fish
2 to 3 tablespoons clarified butter (page 107)

∾ You need three shallow bowls. Crack the eggs into one, and mix them up with a fork. Put the flour in another, and add the salt and pepper. Put the bread crumbs in the third bowl.

∾ First dip a fillet (the part of the fish that has been cut off the bone) in the flour, both sides, and gently shake off any extra. It should be lightly powdered all over. Then dip the floured fish in the egg, both sides, and let the extra drip off. Then lay it in the bread crumbs. Scoop some crumbs from the sides of the bowl and cover the top of the fish. Press down gently all over, then lift from the bowl and set on a plate. Do that for all the fish.

∾ To cook, heat a large sauté or frying pan over medium heat on the stove. Melt the butter, then put in the fish and cook for 3 to 4 minutes until the crumbs are nicely browned. Use a spatula to turn the fish over, and cook another 2 to 3 minutes. The second side cooks faster than the first. As soon as it's done, take it from the pan and serve right away. I like it with lemon.

Fresh Bread Crumbs

Bread crumbs made from fresh, soft bread are delicious. They smell like fresh toast and make foods crunchy and crispy.

❧ Cut the crusts off some slices of bread, then cut the bread into chunks. Put one or two handfuls at a time into a blender, put the top on, and turn it on for about half a minute. Empty it out and do another handful until you have what you need. You can put bags of extra crumbs in the freezer to have ready for another time.

Clarified Butter

Clarified butter (clear butter) is what happens when you separate the butterfat from the milk solids. The white milk solids will burn at a low temperature, so unclarified butter is not good for frying. If they are removed, then the butterfat can cook at a much higher temperature, like vegetable oils but with the flavor of butter.

❧ Gently melt the butter, whatever amount needed. A white foam will float to the top. Tip the pan to the side, and use a spoon to skim the foam off the yellow butter below.

Extra butter can be kept, covered, in the refrigerator for weeks, or the freezer for months.

Chicken

You want to eat a chicken that's been eating good things itself. They're usually the ones that come from farms where they take the best care of their birds and give them lots of room.

Where do you get the most tasty eggs? My friend Zac goes out in his backyard right here in Berkeley and gets them right out from under his family's chickens! I go down to Café Fanny, where they have blue eggs that come from Araucana chickens who have feathers on their feet! Sometimes we go to the farmers' market, where the farmers bring fresh eggs every day.

CHICKEN BROTH

3 to 4 pounds chicken parts: whole chicken; or necks,
   backs, wings; or the remains of roasted chicken
4 quarts cold water
2 carrots, peeled and sliced
1 onion, sliced
1 stalk celery, sliced
1 leek, split lengthwise and rinsed
1 sprig thyme
Handful of parsley sprigs
1 bay leaf
1 teaspoon salt
Black peppercorns

❧ Put the chicken in a large pot, add the water, and bring to a boil. Let it boil gently for 10 to 15 minutes, and use a big, flat spoon to skim off the fat and froth that floats to the top. When it is nice and clear, add the vegetables, herbs, salt, and a few black peppercorns, and lower the heat to a gentle simmer. Let it simmer 2 to 3 hours.

❧ Turn off the heat, and let it cool down a while before you strain it. Here is a good method for straining it: Line a large bowl with 2 plastic bags and use a flat strainer (called a spider) or a big slotted spoon to lift the meat, bones, and vegetables out of the broth and into the plastic bags. The double bags prevent leaks in the garbage.

❧ Then ladle the broth through a fine mesh strainer into containers to store in the freezer. Put in the refrigerator until cold; then you can easily remove the fat that collects at the top before freezing. It will keep in the refrigerator for 3 or 4 days, or for months in the freezer.

You can save extra pieces of chicken, either raw or cooked, in the freezer, and add them to the pot when you make chicken broth.

ROAST CHICKEN WITH HERBS

One 3- to 4-pound chicken
1 teaspoon rosemary, chopped
1 teaspoon thyme, chopped
1 teaspoon oregano or marjoram, chopped
½ teaspoon salt
¼ teaspoon black pepper
1 tablespoon olive oil
1 clove garlic

∽ Rinse the chicken inside and out with cold water. Remove the two pockets of fat just inside the cavity, then pat dry with a towel.

∽ Make an herb paste by mixing the chopped herbs, salt, pepper, olive oil, and garlic. Hold the pointy ends of a fork against a plate and rub the peeled garlic against the tips to make a juicy puree. Rub the paste all over the outside of the chicken.

∽ Set the chicken on a rack in a roasting pan, breast side up, and cook in a 375°F oven for 20 minutes. Then turn the chicken over and cook another 20 minutes, breast side down. Then turn it over again, breast side up, for the last 20 minutes of cooking. If the bird is on the large side, 4 pounds or more, it will need an additional 15 minutes.

∽ When it is cooked, remove from the oven, lightly cover with foil, and let it sit for 15 to 20 minutes. This resting time is very important for all cooked meats so that the texture will be tender and juicy. Before cutting and serving, collect the juices from the roasting pan. skim off the layer of clear fat from the top, and moisten the servings with the tasty juices.

We often have a simple supper of roast or grilled chicken with lettuce vinaigrette and garlic croutons. The chicken juices and the vinaigrette are really good together.

Rice

Rice is grown all over the world. For lots of people it's the most important thing they eat. Here are my favorite kinds of rice: There's jasmine rice that comes from Thailand and smells like flowers, and there's Basmati rice from India that smells sort of grassy and spicy, and there's Arborio rice from Italy that has the very creamiest texture.

Plain Rice

1 cup rice

2 cups water

½ teaspoon salt

∾ Measure 1 cup rice into a saucepan with a tight-fitting lid, and add 2 cups water. Add ½ teaspoon salt if you like. Put on the stove over medium heat and bring to a boil. When it begins to bubble, turn down the heat to very low, give the rice a stir, and cover the pan.

∾ Let it cook for 20 minutes, then turn off the heat, let sit for 4 to 5 minutes, and serve.

RISOTTO

Risotto is a kind of rice that Italians make. They use a special kind called Arborio that soaks up the flavors of anything you cook with it.

3 TO 4 SERVINGS

4 cups chicken broth (1 quart)
1 small onion
1 tablespoon butter
1 tablespoon olive oil
1 bay leaf
1 sprig fresh thyme
Salt and pepper
1 cup Arborio rice, or short-grain white rice
1 tablespoon olive oil
Parmesan cheese

✑ Heat the chicken broth to just boiling. Taste for salt. It should taste salty, so add some if needed.

✑ Peel and chop an onion fine, and put it in a heavy-bottomed saucepan with 1 tablespoon each of butter and olive oil. Add the bay leaf and thyme, and cook gently over medium heat for 4 to 5 minutes until the onions are soft and clear.

✑ Add the rice and cook another 5 minutes, stirring often. Then ladle onto the rice enough hot chicken broth to just cover the rice. You will hear it bubble and hiss at first. Stir the rice, and lower the heat to a very gentle bubbling. Cook, uncovered, for about 10 minutes, until almost all the broth has been absorbed by the rice.

➴ Add the remaining hot broth and continue cooking at a gentle simmer another 10 minutes or so until the rice is tender but just a little chewy at the center. Near the end of the cooking, stir in a tablespoon of olive oil and taste for salt. Add more if needed. One of the special things about risotto is that there should still be some soupy broth in the pot when the rice is done. Serve it right away with some black pepper and freshly grated Parmesan cheese.

You can add many things to a risotto, if you like. Sweet fresh peas and ham, wilted greens, mushrooms, leftover bits of roast chicken or grilled vegetables—whatever you like. Try adding a pinch of saffron threads to the onions for a golden risotto.

Birthday Cake and Treats

Good, ripe fruit is usually all my mom lets me have for dessert, and it doesn't need sugar or anything else. I love fruit, but sometimes it's fun to cook and eat special desserts. And you have to have a birthday cake on your birthday.

1-2-3-4 Cake

This cake is called 1-2-3-4 because it is a very old recipe and people could remember the ingredients by the numbers without having to write it down. This is what we make for birthday cakes. It is very good plain, or with lemon curd and fresh violets.

TWO 8- OR 9-INCH LAYERS

1 cup unsalted butter (2 sticks) at room temperature
2 cups sugar
3 cups cake flour
4 teaspoons baking powder
½ teaspoon salt
4 eggs
1 teaspoon vanilla extract
1 cup milk

∾ Turn on the oven to 350°F. Measure all the ingredients and get organized before you begin to make the batter. The butter should be soft. Cut it into small pieces, and put in a large bowl. Measure the sugar and set aside.

∾ Sift the cake flour, scoop into a measuring cup, scrape a knife across the top of the cup to level it, and measure 3 cups. Put the flour in a separate bowl. Measure level teaspoons of the baking powder and add to the flour. Measure the salt and add to the flour. Mix together.

∾ Separate the eggs. Put the whites in one bowl and the yolks in another. Have the vanilla ready, and measure the milk and set aside.

∾ Butter the insides of two 8- or 9-inch cake pans. Rub a small amount of butter all over the inside; don't miss the corners. Then put a tablespoon or so of flour in the pan and turn it all around so the pan is completely dusted with flour. Turn the pan upside down, and tap the edge on the table to let the extra flour fall out.

∾ Now everything is ready to make the batter. Beat the butter with a wooden spoon or in a mixer until light and fluffy. Add the sugar and beat again until very fluffy and light yellow. This is what it means to *cream* the butter and sugar. Add the egg yolks and beat them in briefly. Add 1 teaspoon vanilla and mix it in well.

∾ Next add the flour and milk in parts. Sift about half of the flour over the butter mixture and lightly stir it in. Exchange the spoon for a large rubber spatula, and pour in about half the milk. Use the spatula to gently mix the milk into the batter. Sift over the rest of the flour and stir it in. Pour in the rest of the milk and gently mix it in.

∾ The last step is to beat the egg whites and fold them into the batter. Put the egg whites into a very clean metal bowl, and beat with a whisk or mixer. They will gradually thicken and get very white as you beat in air bubbles. When the whites are very fluffy and will hold a soft peak shape when you lift up the whisk, they're ready.

∾ Scoop up some of the whites with the spatula, add to the batter, and very gently stir them in. This will lighten the batter and make it easier to fold in the rest of the whites. Then pour the rest of the whites onto the batter and begin to fold them in. Folding is more delicate than stirring. Use the spatula to lift up some of the batter from the bottom of the bowl and fold it over the whites. Turn the bowl a little and fold again. Do that just until the egg whites are mixed in. The air bubbles in the whites will give the cake a light and delicate texture.

∾ Divide the batter between the cake pans, and put in the center of the oven to bake for about 25 minutes. When the cakes are lightly browned, and a toothpick stuck in the center comes out clean, they're done. Remove from the oven and cool on a rack.

You can cut the recipe in half to make a single layer cake. Or a full recipe will make 32 cupcakes—fill the papers half full.

Vanilla Snow

This tastes like vanilla ice cream and feels like snow.

3 CUPS

> 1½ cups milk
> ½ cup half-and-half
> 6 tablespoons sugar
> 1-inch piece vanilla bean
> ¼ cup egg whites (2 large eggs)
> 1 tablespoon sugar

❧ In a small bowl, combine the milk, half-and-half, and 6 tablespoons sugar. Cut the vanilla bean in half the long way, and scrape out the tiny black seeds inside. Add the bean and the scrapings to the milk mixture. Stir with a spoon until the sugar is dissolved.

❧ Put the egg whites into a clean metal bowl, and beat them with a whisk or beater until they are thick and white and will hold the shape of soft peaks when you lift up the whisk. Add 1 tablespoon sugar to the whites and beat until they form stiff peaks.

❧ Remove the vanilla bean from the milk mixture. (If you let it dry, it can be used again for something else.) Add the egg whites to the milk mixture, and use a spatula to gently fold the two together. You can use a whisk to gently break up any large bits of whites. Freeze the mixture in an ice-cream freezer according to the directions.

Plum Ice Cream

1½ cups plum puree (about 1 pound plums)
1 cup plus 2 tablespoons sugar
2 cups whipping cream
½ cup sugar
½ teaspoon vanilla extract

❧ Puree ripe, tasty plums by cooking them until soft, and passing them through a food mill or pureeing them in a food processor. Measure 1½ cups of puree and put it in a bowl, add 1 cup and 2 tablespoons sugar, and stir until the sugar is dissolved. It is best to do this while the puree is still warm, but it can be done when it is cool.

❧ Put the cream in another bowl and add the remaining ½ cup sugar and the vanilla. Stir until the sugar is dissolved. Combine both mixtures and stir well. Freeze in an ice-cream freezer according to the directions.

GINGERSNAPS

½ pound unsalted butter (2 sticks) at room temperature

1 cup plus 6 tablespoons sugar

½ teaspoon vanilla extract

1 egg

1/3 cup molasses

3 cups all-purpose flour

½ teaspoon salt

1½ teaspoons cinnamon

1½ teaspoons powdered ginger

❧ Turn on the oven to 350°F. The butter should be soft. Put it in a large bowl and beat it with a wooden spoon or in a mixer until light and fluffy. Add the sugar, and beat it into the butter until light and fluffy again. This is what it means to *cream* the butter and the sugar. Add the vanilla, egg, and molasses, and continue creaming until all is mixed well. In another bowl, mix together the flour, salt, cinnamon, and ginger. Add to the butter mixture and mix well.

❧ Divide the dough into 3 equal pieces, wrap the pieces in plastic wrap, and chill for about 30 minutes. On a lightly floured board, roll each piece of dough into a log-shaped cylinder about 1¾ inches across. Wrap the logs in plastic, and place in the freezer for 20 or 30 minutes until firm.

❧ Line a cookie sheet with parchment paper. Slice the logs into cookies about ¼ inch thick and place on the cookie sheet, leaving about 2 inches between each cookie. Sprinkle the tops with sugar, if you like. Bake the cookies for 8 to 10 minutes. Let the cookies cool a bit before removing them from the pan. You can reuse the same parchment to bake the next batch of cookies.

For Plum Ice Cream Sandwiches: Place a scoop of plum ice cream (page 121) onto a gingersnap, top it with another, and press together. Wrap in plastic, and store in the freezer.

Candied Orange Peel

This is not only for oranges. You can candy other kinds of citrus peels: tangerines, lemons, limes, grapefruit, and tangelos.

1½ TO 2 CUPS

    4 oranges
    1 cup sugar
    ½ cup water
    Granulated sugar

༛ Put a large saucepan of water on the stove to boil. Cut the oranges in half and juice them. You can drink the juice while you prepare the peels. Cut the halves in two and pull out the pulp.

༛ Gently boil the peels for 5 minutes or so until the white pith on the inside of the skin is quite soft and yellow. Drain and cool the peels. Use a spoon to scrape away the pith, being careful not to tear the peels. Cut the peels into thin strips.

༛ Mix the sugar and ½ cup water in a saucepan and put on the stove over medium heat. When the sugar is dissolved, add the strips of peel. Stir now and then until the peels and syrup begin to boil. Let them boil gently for 5 minutes, then turn off the heat and let them sit in the pan for 24 hours.

༛ The next day, heat the syrup and peels to boiling again. Stir now and then, and boil gently until the syrup cooks to the thread stage, about 10 minutes. You can test this by dipping a spoon or fork in the syrup, lifting it out, and watching the syrup drip. When the drips leave a thread of sugar as they fall, it's ready. Right away, drain the peels in a strainer.

When the peels are cool, separate them and toss in some granulated sugar until lightly coated; shake off the extra. Store in an airtight container.

They are delicious just by themselves, but sometimes we dip the ends in melted chocolate and then set them on a plate to cool. The cooks at the restaurant like to chop them up to put into pies and tarts, ice creams, and on top of cakes and custards.

Chocolate Kisses

3¼ ounces best quality semi-sweet chocolate
1 tablespoon cold unsalted butter

❧ Chop the chocolate, and put it in a small metal bowl over a pot of water heated to just barely bubbling. Gently stir the chocolate until it has melted. Remove the bowl from the pan, and add the butter cut into small pieces. Stir until the butter has melted. The mixture will be stiff. Allow it to cool enough so that the kisses will stand up when you shape them.

❧ Spoon the chocolate into a small plastic sandwich bag, squeezing it into a corner of the bag. Cut the tip of the corner of the bag when you are ready to squeeze out the kisses. Line a baking sheet with parchment paper or wax paper. Squeeze out the chocolate into kisses about ¾-inch across onto the paper. Put in the refrigerator to cool. Wrap the kisses in foil or cellophane.

Menus

Sometimes I put the recipes together
and make up whole meals. These
are some of my favorite ones.

My Birthday

Cherry Tomato
Pasta

1-2-3-4 Cake

Class Pizza Party

Vegetables Vinaigrette

Colored Peppers Pizza

Blackberry
Ice Cream

Tisane

SPRING

Cucumber Raita
with Pooris

Golden Risotto

Vanilla Snow

SUMMER

Tomato Salad

Halibut Baked
on a Fig Leaf

Peach Crisp

FALL

Carrot and Parsley
Salad

Lemon Sole Fried
with Bread Crumbs

Green and Purple Figs

WINTER

Lettuce Greens
with Vinaigrette

Roast Chicken
with Herbs
Polenta

Golden Delicious
Applesauce

129

Index

ALICE WATERS is Fanny's mother. She is the founder and proprietor of Chez Panisse, a restaurant and café in Berkeley, California. Among the books Alice Waters and her colleagues have produced are *Chez Panisse Cooking* (by Paul Bertoli), *Chez Panisse Pasta, Pizza & Calzone* (with Patricia Curtan and Martin Labro), *Chez Panisse Desserts* (by Lindsey Shere), *The Chez Panisse Menu Cookbook*, and *Chez Panisse Vegetables*.

BOB CARRAU is a writer and screenwriter who lives in San Francisco.

PATRICIA CURTAN is an artist and book designer who lives in Berkeley and who cooked for many years at Chez Panisse.

ANN ARNOLD is a still-life painter who lives around the corner from Chez Panisse.